PROLOGUE

It was 2:00 in the morning and I was standing on the beach, blindfolded and shivering in the night air. I tried to listen to what was going on around me so that I could get some idea of what was going to happen but all I could hear was the sound of the waves crashing very close to where I was standing. I tried to hear sounds coming from my sister or brothers that would let me know that they were ok but, again, all I could hear was the ocean. I wanted to speak, no, I wanted to scream out and yell at him and ask him what was happening; but I knew better. When we were told to do something we did it, with no questions asked because if we didn't, the consequences would always be brutal. My mind was racing and I was trying to figure out how to get out of this predicament. I couldn't figure out why we were standing at the edge of the ocean, in the middle of the night. I kept going over the entire day in my head and asking myself what I or one of my siblings could have done that had finally pushed him over the edge. With the roar of the ocean in my ears, the only conclusion I could come to was that one or more of us had finally angered him to the point that he had decided to bring us out here in the middle of the night and drown us. I am not sure if I was afraid or looking forward to ending the madness that was my life. Then I started thinking about the fact that there were five of us and there was no way he could drown all five of us at the same time so I started to devise a plan. I was the oldest and it was up to me to figure a way out of this. I figured if I grabbed the baby and started running and just kept running until I found help that I could save at least two of us and maybe put an end to this madness. Finally I heard my mother speak up and tell him that he had to stop because we were too afraid. Even though I could not see his face through my blindfold, I could feel his fury and held my breath to see what would happen next. I felt him pick me up and throw me in the back of the truck and when all five of us were in the truck together, I heard the door slam and then the driver and passenger doors slam and the truck started up. I breathed a sigh of relief because once more we had made it through another one of his initiations. It was 1964; I was 7 years old.

Chocolate or Vanilla

When writing about something that happened during childhood, how do make sure you are writing about facts and not what you perceive to be the truth? This book, to the best of my knowledge, is factual – based on events as I perceived them through the eyes of my childhood. My apologies to anyone involved that may have perceived any of the events in this book differently than I did.

ACKNOWLEDGMENTS

This book is dedicated to my brother Michael, I love you Meo and dread to think of where I would be without your love and guidance because the student has become the teacher. Aunt Mary Lou and Aunt Judy, I am who I am today because you are in my life. My beautiful daughters, you continue to be the best gift I have ever received. Andrew, thank you for the way you love my daughter and for my grandson. And to Anthony, because your love, imagination and intelligence make everything I have experienced worth my journey just to have you in my life! You teach me something valuable every time I am with you and through you my life has meaning!

Chocolate or Vanilla

I have asked myself if I should write this book because the content is bound to affect many people in different ways. Those of us that lived through it will be affected differently than those who may find something in its pages to encourage them to find their Inner Strength. If there is one thing I have learned, keeping quiet, when something needs to be brought out into the open, helps no one. Speaking up is difficult and can cause much heartache on many levels. I promise you, the truth shall set you free.

When I meet someone that has lived an idyllic childhood, I am always amazed at the wonderful memories they have to share. Likewise, when I share my childhood memories, people often find the facts hard to believe and are downright skeptical because it is difficult to believe that such occurrences take place. We don't want to believe that children suffer the way they do and we really don't want to believe that it has happened to someone we know. It is this "head in the sand" mentality that makes it difficult for a child to speak up. The most important gift you can give a child is to "hear" them. You may not have the answer for them, but if they know they are being heard, they will know they are not alone.

Chocolate or Vanilla

Our deepest fear is not that we are inadequate. Our deepest fear is that we are powerful beyond measure. It is our light, not our darkness that most frightens us. We ask ourselves "who am I to be brilliant, gorgeous, talented, fabulous?"
Actually, who are you not to be?
You are a child of God. Your playing small does not serve the world. There is nothing enlightened about shrinking so that other people will not feel insecure around you. We are all meant to shine, as children do. We were born to make manifest the glory of God that is within us. It is not just in some of us, it is in everyone. And as we let our own light shine, we unconsciously give others permission to do the same. As we are liberated from our own fear, our presence liberates others.
– Marianne Williamson

Chocolate or Vanilla

Over the years, after hearing parts of my life's journey, many people have suggested that I write a book to share my story. I have read and heard stories of many amazing women over the years and I am sharing my story not because I am so amazing, but because I believe that I have been given a gift and I would like to share my gift with you.

This is not a motivational book, or a self-help book or even a book to tell you how to reach your goals. This book is my journey to New Beginnings, how I chose to break the cycle of where I came from and how I got where I am. My wish is that something I have written will give you the strength to keep moving forward and empower you to believe that you can be or do anything, regardless of where you come from.

My childhood was full of fear and self-loathing and it took many years for me to realize the gift that I had been given was my Inner Strength and how it would serve me through good times and through challenging times. I am honored for this opportunity to share my story with you in the hope that you will look beyond the person, embrace the optimism, and believe that your past is not who you are. You can change your past by changing your choices in the present. Live in the present, live in *"the now."*

Chocolate or Vanilla

When we can see someone for who they are and not where they came from we honor their presence.

Never be envious of what someone else has because you do not know the price they paid to get it!

Chapter 1

My mother was raised on a 40-acre farm in Canton, Ohio consisting of a two bedroom house, with 7 siblings; 4 boys and 4 girls. With only 2 bedrooms and 8 children this meant that my mother and her brothers and sisters often shared the same bedroom, with the youngest sleeping between my grandparents. My grandparents were from Italy and both were hard working people that worked just as hard on the farm as they did raising their children and working in the local factory. My grandfather ruled the house with an iron fist, a loud voice and little compassion. My grandmother was very quiet and the backbone of the home and my mother rarely left the farm except to attend school.

When my father proposed to my mother she thought that her prince had come and that he would take her away from the farm, move her to sunny California and start a whole new life near my father's family. The day after the wedding my parents left Ohio for California, and spent their honeymoon traveling west. My mother was young, naïve, and had romantic ideas of her new life in California. Reality quickly set in during that trip to California when her dreams of starting a romantic life with her new husband gave her a rude awakening and she realized that she had made a terrible mistake by marrying my father. And worse, she could not go back.

Her first clue was the fact that my father couldn't wait to get to on the road because he had read somewhere of a ranch in Oklahoma where men could have sex with sheep. All my mother could think about was "what was she supposed to do while her husband was having sex with animals?" He never found the sheep ranch but when they arrived in California the romance my mother had dreamed of, quickly turned to grief. My mother had 5 children within the first six years of her marriage and never had the opportunity to find out who she was, let alone grasp the concept of proper parenting or enjoying the birth of each child.

How did a woman in the 1960's with 5 children, a sex addicted abusive husband (who did not want to work) with very little hope for the future of her children, and who only knew her own fear and self-doubt, raise her children?

If you were my mother, you screamed, cried, were verbally abusive to her children, and thought that if you kept your children as quiet as possible you were doing the right thing, because a beating from her was far better than a beating we children would receive from our father.

Chapter 2

One of the things I never understood was why my mother didn't intervene and protect us from our father's abuse. It wasn't until years later when I asked her that question that she told me that he used to tell her if she didn't do exactly as he wanted, he would leave her and she would have to find a way to take care of her five children by herself. She used to think that she was helping us by yelling and screaming at us to keep us in line. She thought that if she could make us strong that she was "making us tough."

Whenever my mother used to serve ice cream she would ask us, "do you want chocolate or vanilla?" If we said we wanted chocolate, she would give us vanilla. If we said we wanted vanilla she would give us chocolate. If we thought we were smarter than her and told her we wanted chocolate (when we really wanted vanilla) she would give us chocolate.

Chocolate or Vanilla

We could never figure out how to get what we wanted and she assumed she was teaching us how to deal with disappointment.

My father could never make up his mind where he wanted to live so we constantly moved back and forth from California to Ohio and back again.

Because he did not want to work, it meant that we never had any money. There also never seemed to be enough food and we were always hungry. My mother did not work outside of the home and taking care of five children was her full time job. As a mother, being able to feed and clothe her children was always her main concern. Our food and clothing were often supplied to us from whatever church we were currently attending. We also relied heavily on relatives and hand-me-downs from anywhere we could get them. Being poor is one thing; being poor because your husband doesn't want to work is something else entirely for a wife and mother to deal with.

Our father's lack of work also meant that we often lived with different relatives. When I was in kindergarten we lived with my father's parents in a 3 bedroom house, which meant that there were 13 people living in their house with only one bathroom. At Christmas we would watch our cousins get presents wrapped in bright paper with pretty bows. Like most children, my siblings and I believed in Santa Claus, it was difficult for our mother to make us understand why there were no presents under the tree for us.

Chocolate or Vanilla

Chapter 3

When my sister was being abused, it never occurred to me to try to come to her rescue; quite the opposite, actually. I would be happy the abuse was not directed at me and I would try to find ways to also abuse her.

My thinking was that if it made my dad happy to abuse her, then he would be happy if I were doing the same thing.

One day my father was mad at my sister and decided to punish her. He tied her to a post in our kitchen, pulled her shirt up to her shoulders, put water on her stomach and then rubbed salt all over her wet stomach. He kept pounding her stomach and rubbing the salt into her skin because he wanted her to admit to something she did wrong. My sister just stood there, tied to the post, staring off at something only she could see the whole time this took place. I watched her stomach get redder and redder as the skin was rubbed raw from the salt. It never occurred to me to try to come to her rescue; on the contrary, I was glad it was her and not me.

Being glad his attention was directed towards my sister instead of me was usually short lived, because sooner or later he would turn his sadistic thoughts to both of us at the same time by making us fight each other. Fighting each other meant that when the fight was over, one of us was the winner, and one of us was the loser. There was never an option for me to say that I didn't want to fight because that would mean he would find a way to take his anger out on me. I would much rather take my chances with my sister than with him so I fought her until there was a winner; and I *NEVER* lost. To this day, my sister has the scars, both mentally and physically, to prove that she always lost the fight. As a child, trying to survive in my world, victory seemed the most important thing to be proud of. It never occurred to me what harm I might be doing to my sister. I thought that winning a fight meant that I was strong and losing a fight meant that I was weak. I learned that when you are weak, you get hurt, when you are strong, you get hurt less.

Chocolate or Vanilla

My father never tied me to a pole; instead he seemed to favor beating me with a fiberglass fishing rod. He used to store the fishing rod over the door jamb leading into the kitchen. I used to think about ways that I could destroy the fishing rod or throw it in the trash but was more afraid of what would happen to me *if* I touched it, than how much it hurt to get hit with it. I already knew what it felt like to get hit with the fishing rod. Not knowing what he would dream up if I got caught getting rid of it was worse. The anticipation and fear of the unknown, was almost worse than the actual event. If you knew what was coming, you could mentally prepare for it. The unknown would cause a fear that would grip my mind so tightly; I would find myself wishing I would just die so I wouldn't have to deal with it. In fact, death was something I found myself praying for quite often in the years to come. I truly felt that I meant nothing to anyone and no one was going to save us.

I grew up in the era of Bruce Lee and I used to believe that if I could just learn to defend myself, like Bruce, my troubles would be over and no one would ever touch me again. Beatings with the fishing rod would strip my dignity, and then he got more creative and stripped my clothes to beat me naked in front of the rest of the family. I lost dignity as well as hope that anyone would intervene.

When my father used to strip me naked and beat me with that fiberglass fishing rod, I used to fantasize about using Karate to get out of the situation. In my fantasy, I would use the fiberglass fishing rod on him, to show him how it felt, and then I would break it so he would respect my knowledge to protect myself and he would never come near me again.

But that was only a fantasy in my head, so the beatings continued, my dignity dwindled, my fear grew and I believed that I meant nothing to anyone.

Chapter 4

When I was in the 6th grade, my great-grandmother died so we went to live with our great-grandfather, on my father's side of the family. Gramps lived in Ohio and since there were only 3 bedrooms my brothers had to sleep in the attic. We moved in during the summer and the attic seemed like the perfect retreat for my sister, brothers, and I to stay out of the way. Our retreat seemed less welcoming as winter approached because there was no heat in the attic and in the winter it got very cold.

My mom would often send all 5 of us to the attic when she wanted us out of the way during one of my father's moods. I would feel bad telling my brothers "good night," knowing that I could walk downstairs to my warm room while they were huddled under the covers trying to keep warm. Sometimes, when going downstairs meant possibly

Chocolate or Vanilla

running into my dad I would opt to huddle under the covers with my brothers and sleep in the attic.

During our stay at my great-grandfather's house my father talked more and more about wanting to leave my mother. She could not stand the thought of being left alone with 5 children and having to raise us in our great-grandfather's house. Lucky for her, our great-grandfather lived across the street from the local hospital; my mother decided to apply for a job and was hired. This could have been considered good news for my mother, but more importantly it meant that I had to be more responsible for my siblings.

While our mother worked, it was up to me to take care of my sister and brothers and get them off to school. Since they attended the grade school only a block away, we would all walk to school together. I would drop them off and continue walking another half mile to the junior high school. This was the first time I had ever lived in the city and nothing was familiar to me. I felt all alone and scared, walking to school with no one to know if I arrived safe and sound. On my first day at the junior high I saw my first fight between two female students. The girls were going after each other, scratching and clawing, and I remember thinking that it was the first time I had seen two girls fight other than my sister and I. My first thought at my new school was that I hoped I would not have to fight my way out of any situations at school.

Chocolate or Vanilla

Chapter 5

The following spring, my mother's father died, so (again) we moved. This time we moved in with our grandmother, in the home where my mother grew up.

My grandmother still lived on the same 40-acre farm in a small two-bedroom house so my siblings and I slept outside in a tent during the summer months and when winter arrived, we slept inside the house on the living room floor.

I was 12 years old, I loved my grandmother, our dad was rarely home so life seemed good. Our father seemed to be away a lot and in the mornings my mom would wake us up for school by playing music on the record player to get us up and moving for the day. We would listen to Bobby Sherman, The Partridge Family, Patsy Cline, Neil Diamond and Elvis. Life seemed to finally be calming down

Chocolate or Vanilla

and the abuse from my father was practically non-existent due to the fact that my grandma was in the house.

One summer day, when my mom and my grandmother were away at work, my father sent my sister and brothers outside to play, with strict instructions not to come back in the house until he gave them permission. They knew better than to argue or request permission to go back in the house, even if they had to use the bathroom, so off they went to play in the yard. I was told to stay in the house, work on my chores and my father told me he was going to go take a bath.

A little while later, my father called out to me and told me he wanted to see me. I walked into the bedroom and found him sitting, naked, on the bed. He told me to sit on the bed beside him. As he started talking to me, his breathing changed, and then he pushed me back on the bed and took my clothes off of me. His breathing was heavy and he told me that he needed to teach me something very important. He told me that if any boy or man tried to touch me the way he was touching me that it was wrong and that I should not allow it.

The events that took place after he removed my clothes will be forever seared into my memory from the beginning of the attack until the end, when I had to clean the bedspread to get rid of any evidence of what had taken place.

Afterward, I was so confused, scared, repulsed, and afraid. He kept telling me over and over that I could not tell anyone what had happened. He told me that if I ever told anyone that he would get into a lot of trouble. I could sense that his fear of getting into trouble made him angry and his anger was something I wanted to avoid at all cost.

I soon realized that there was no help for what had just happened, but my bigger concern was finding a way to keep it from happening again. While I was trying to keep my distance, luck was with me. My father's youngest brother decided to surprise our family with a visit and stayed with us at the farm for a few months. Since my uncle was around during the day, I was spared any more visits from my father for the next few months.

After my uncle returned to California, my parents bought a home and our family moved into our own house. Within the first month our father began regularly bringing his "lady friend" over for dinner. She would sit at our table and have dinner with us and I always wondered who this mysterious lady was.

Chocolate or Vanilla

Two months later, in mid-October of my 8th grade school year, my father left my mother and ran off with his "lady friend". I came home from school one day to find my mother's wedding dress, pictures, and other memories in the trash can. My mother had tried to do everything my father demanded, but in the end, he left her anyway, with 5 children and no financial support.

My father was gone, but I had jumped from the frying pan into the fire. At that point, my mother went after me with everything she had. She would constantly scream at me and tell me that "I looked just like my father, I acted just like my father and the sight of me made her sick!" She worked; I went to school, came home, cooked, cleaned, did the laundry, ironed, cared for my siblings and assumed the role of mother and homemaker. I was 14 years old.

If my mother would come home from work to find me napping on the couch, she would pull me by the hair until I fell off the couch and scream at me for not completing my chores. There was little time to think about homework and no time to be a kid.

Chapter 6

My mother remarried in December of my freshman year in high school. I started spending as much time as possible with another family that had a girl my age and they welcomed me into their family. There was such a difference in the home lives between their home and mine. When I cleaned or helped with laundry, her mom used to thank me. And there was always plenty to eat.

I used to eat so much when I was at their house that I was embarrassed at how much food I could eat compared to her children. They would eat one donut and be full; I would eat 2 and sneak 2 more. It amazed me that they always seemed to have an abundance of food and that no one was rationed on how much food they were allowed to eat. I lived with this family every weekend and any day during the week that I could get a ride to their house.

Chocolate or Vanilla

The down side of me being away so much was that there was no one to cook and clean for my siblings. My sister would try to cook and bake, but it was not one of her strengths. My brothers missed me terribly. It was a definite push/pull situation for me because I loved the freedom of staying with the other family, but felt bad for my brothers. When I would be at home my mother was always screaming at me or slapping me around so I really did not want to be there. During my sophomore year, while still married to her second husband, my mother changed jobs and met a man she would have an on-again off-again affair with for the next 36 years.

Chocolate or Vanilla

Chapter 7

Many people assumed I got married at a young age because I wanted to get out of the house. Actually, I was married at age 17 simply because that seemed like the next logical step for me. I had been taking care of my siblings, cooking, cleaning, doing laundry, ironing and being the main caregiver in our home. I had been taking care of people since I was six years old; there was no opportunity to have a childhood or learn who I was, what I wanted to become or who I wanted to be with. I thought that if I found a man that wanted to marry me and he didn't hit me and didn't have affairs, then I would have chosen a good husband. I was wrong! I had yet to learn the importance of choosing a partner that shared my core values.

I really wanted to be a teacher but my mother could not stand the sight of me, my grades were not good enough to qualify for college, nor was there money for college. Living on my own was not an option and the truth was that I really did not believe I was smart enough to be a teacher. From kindergarten through high school I attended 13 different schools. We moved so often that it was next to impossible to keep friends or even pay attention in school. It seemed useless to try to learn anything because just about the time that I would get interested in something we would move and then I would have to start all over again.

When a child is told something often enough, soon he or she believes it to be true. I was told that I was worthless, that I would never amount to anything, that I was trash, and, more often than I can count; my mother used to scream at me that she should have thrown me away and kept the afterbirth.

Chocolate or Vanilla

The spiritual meaning of every situation is not what happens to us, but what we do with what happens to us and who we decide to become because of what happens to us. The only real failure is the failure to grow from what we go through.

- Marianne Williamson

Chapter 8

Looking back, I realize that the best thing I had going for me was the Inner Strength to survive. Often I would fantasize about changing my home life and I would relive the negative situation, in my mind, so that it ended in a positive way. Little did I realize at the time, but this was the start of my initiation into the power of positive thoughts.

Whenever I would start to dwell on what was happening to me at home I would read about children that were treated far worse than I was and I would be thankful that my abuse paled in comparison to what they were suffering. You can always take a negative situation and find a way to think positively.

Sometimes you might really have to dig deep, but eventually you will find something to be thankful for. Today, I am the most positive person I know and it

Chocolate or Vanilla

is this positive energy that I feel is the gift that I have been given to share with others. It is this positive energy that I call my "Inner Strength."

Don't Quit!

When things go wrong, as they sometimes will,
when the road you're trudging seems uphill,
When the funds are low and the debts are high,
And you want to smile, but you have to sigh,
When care is pressing you down a bit,
Rest, if you must, but do not quit.

Life is queer with its twists and turns,
As every one of us sometimes learns,
And many a failure turns about,
When he might have won had he stuck it out;
Don't give up though the pace seems slow
You may succeed with another blow.

Often the goal is nearer than,
It seems to a faint and faltering man,
Often the struggler has given up,
When he might have captured the victors cup,
And he learned too late when the night slipped down,
How close he was to the golden crown.

Success is failure turned inside out
The silver tint of the clouds of doubt,
And you never can tell how close you are,
It may be near when it seems so far,
So stick to the fight when you're hardest hit
Its when things seem worst that you must not quit.

Anonymous

Chapter 9

Drugs were so readily available in my high school and I watched my classmates tripping on LSD, smoking pot and getting wasted every day. I had so many opportunities to withdraw from life and crawl into a world of drugs but something told me that I would be trading a life of self loathing for a life of self destruction and that felt like the wrong path to take. I would watch girls in my class trying to climb the walls in the bathroom to get away from some horrible scene that only they could see, during an acid trip, and I would think, "My life might be crap, but if I take drugs, it will be worse than crap." I believe my Inner Strength protected me even before I knew what it was!

During my junior year I enrolled in a vocational food preparation class so I could do what I loved best; cook and bake. By the end of my junior year I decided to give that up and take secretarial courses to get out of school early by joining the school work program and get married.

During my senior year in high school, while everyone else was looking forward to prom and football games, I used my time in study hall to sew my wedding veil. I had been working for the past 2 years saving my money and planning my wedding day. I graduated the first week of June and 2 weeks later I was married with a traditional Italian reception complete with band, food, and drinks.

We honeymooned in Niagara Falls and when we got back and settled into our lives the first taste of freedom for me was food. I could go to the grocery store and buy food, cook, bake, and eat whatever I wanted and no one rationed what I ate. It felt so wonderful to have plenty of food on the table, in the refrigerator and in the cupboards. I invited my brothers over and I cooked for them and we celebrated our freedom to be together and enjoy each other's company away from the oppressive atmosphere of my mother's house. I always felt so guilty when it was time to take my brothers home. I often wished I could find a way to keep them with me because even though I did not visit my mother's house, I needed to be with my brothers.

One day when I stopped by to pick up my brothers, one of them was bruised and his face was black and blue. I asked him what happened and he told me he had hit a tree while riding his motorcycle. It wasn't until later that he finally confessed that my mother's second husband had been abusing my mother, sister and my brothers. My mother finally forced him to move out when he aimed a shotgun at my sister after he found out that my mother was having an affair with a guy at work. I was horrified; how could all of this be happening and my brothers never told me? We had all been brought up to keep secrets and since I was no longer living in my mother's house, they kept her secret from me. They had kept our mother's secret about seeing another man and when her husband found out my sister almost paid for it with her life.

Chapter 10

It wasn't until after I got married that I finally worked up the courage to tell my husband that my father had molested me. Once I spoke the words out loud and the earth did not open up and swallow me and God did not strike me dead, I felt liberated. I found that I could talk about it without feeling like I had done something wrong and I started to feel less self loathing. Then I finally worked up the courage to tell my mother. When I told her she just stood there and said, "I knew it, that son of a bitch, I knew it." I just looked at her and then asked her, "If you knew what he was doing to me, why didn't you help me?" She just looked at me and said, "What was I going to do? I had five kids. If I tried to go against him; he would have left me alone with you five kids."

I just looked at her and said, "He left you anyway, you should have helped me." Then my mother looked at me and said "you have no idea what I

Chocolate or Vanilla

have gone through to raise you five kids" and at that moment, I knew I was still on my own.

Chapter 11

My husband and I bought our first home and I had my brothers over as much as possible to help me paint and fix it up. It felt good to be surrounded by my brothers and so much freedom. When I found out I was pregnant it was the happiest day of my life; but in my fourth month I miscarried twins.

I was devastated beyond belief because all I ever wanted was to be a mom and to shower love and affection on my children to right all of the wrongs that were done to me during my childhood.

Not long after my miscarriage I got pregnant again only to miscarry a second time. This was such a low point in my life. I was sad, I was lonely, I had no one to talk to about losing my babies and I wanted to be a mom more than anything in my life. I felt that God was punishing me and that I truly must be a bad person if He would not see fit to let me be a mother.

Chapter 12

That fall, my husband lost his job and we decided to sell our house and move to California. It was time for a New Beginning. Besides, my brothers had been sent to California to live with our father and I wanted to be near them.

Several months after moving to California we bought another home and I became pregnant with my oldest daughter. The day that she was born was the day that I first started to believe that I was meant for something great in my life. She was the most perfect baby and my brothers were so excited to have a niece. I was a mom, my brothers were there and on my daughter's first birthday I learned that I was pregnant with my second daughter. I was so worried that I would not have enough love inside me for two children, but on the day that my second daughter was born I felt complete.

Chocolate or Vanilla

I had brought two beautiful healthy girls into this world and I vowed that no one would ever lay a hand on them. I believed that my girls were my shining joy and their childhood would allow me to right all the wrongs from my childhood. These two precious baby girls became my life and I felt as though they were the best gifts I had ever been given.

At the time, I felt that I must be truly special to have been given two such beautiful gifts. I finally understood what it meant to love and to be loved, unconditionally. They loved me because I loved them and I honored them by creating a childhood for them to show them that they were precious, loved, cherished, and very special.

Every day I promised myself that I would do my best to honor them and make their lives better than mine. And I did. I worked hard to make sure they would never know anger, self loathing, hunger, hurt, or fear. I made it my mission that they would feel loved, secure, beautiful, safe, and know that they could *be* or *do* anything they wanted!

I chose to be a stay-at-home mom because I wanted to be there for them and share every day with them. When my oldest daughter started kindergarten, the three of us would walk to school together. I volunteered in her class and my youngest would sit at one of the desks and had the advantage of absorbing what her older sister was learning.

Suddenly I realized how important it was for me to learn how to parent, how to eat right, what to feed them, how to encourage them to excel in school. I also started to understand how important school is and what it means to have a parent that is involved in their lives and encouraged them to study and make the most out of school. My quest for knowledge knew no bounds and I kept seeking to better myself and in turn be the best mother I knew how to be. I wanted my daughters to grow up to believe in themselves, to know how much I loved them and how proud I was of them.

Chocolate or Vanilla

Chapter 13

I have always been a great cook and loved to bake. And everyone loved my cookies. One Christmas my neighbor suggested that I bake cookies and she would sell them. She told me that however many cookies I made, she would go out and sell them and we could split the proceeds. So I went out and bought all of the ingredients and an upright freezer. I started baking in November, froze the cookies and when Christmas got closer my neighbor started selling them. When every last cookie was sold and she took her portion of the proceeds, I paid off the freezer and still had $800 profit! I felt on top of the world because I had earned money for something that I was really good at doing and it felt empowering!

The following spring, I was introduced to a multi-level marketing company selling supplements and I was excited at the concept of being able to work from home, be with my girls and earn money at the same time. It was also the beginning of my education into health and the importance of what we put into our bodies. I diligently worked at that business for over a year until it became apparent that I would not excel in that business for 2 reasons: number one, because, although I diligently took the supplements and gave them to my family, I did not feel differently. My energy level did not increase, I still fought my weight and we were always fighting colds. When I asked my upline about this they kept telling me, "Don't worry, you are doing healthy things for your body. Just keep going."

And number two, because I did not *feel* any different, it felt like a lie for me to talk others into joining my business. I felt this way because I was trying to sell something I really didn't believe in. I soon realized that the only person making money off of my business were the people in my upline! I soon gave up the idea of working from home and went to work, part time, as a bookkeeper in a major grocery store chain. I was fortunate because I was often able to take my girls to work with me. I didn't feel so bad about working outside of the home when they could be with me. Soon I began to excel at work and was promoted. I kept working harder and my work was recognized. I continued to move up the ladder of success. I was now in my 30's and very proud of my career accomplishments, considering the fact that I barely graduated from high school!

Chapter 14

I credit two major events in my life for the woman I am today; studying Martial Arts and being introduced to the self-esteem work by Jack Canfield. It wasn't until my late 30's that I finally had the opportunity to start studying Karate. When I finally got up the courage, I entered the dojo and walked up to the instructor and asked, "If I take your class, are you going to throw me on the floor?" He looked very surprised and said "do you want me to?" I said, "No." He said, "Ok then, I won't." At this point, I think it is important to tell you that I am the most UN-Sports person I know. To this day I can never remember how many innings are in a football game! When I told my family that I decided to take Karate lessons; I am sure you can understand their skepticism. But, I had come this far, and nothing was going to change my mind. I took out my checkbook and signed up right then and there!

Finally, I was living my dream; I was learning Karate! In the beginning I started out with one class a week but I loved it so much that I started attending twice a week, then six days a week.

When the time came for me to test for my yellow belt and move from white belt to yellow belt, I was very nervous because I had studied so hard and it was important for me to pass. I passed the test and I was extremely proud of my new yellow belt. Achieving that goal, made me want to work harder for the next belt.

I entered my first Karate tournament as a yellow belt and took first place. That trophy meant everything to me, not because I took first place, but because I had the courage to compete. I had pushed myself so far out of my comfort zone to compete, I remember being so nervous, I thought I would throw up all over the judges when I stepped into the ring to present myself.

After yellow belt came orange belt and I flew to Maui to compete at my new rank. There was no stopping me; my thirst for knowledge of the Martial Arts could not be quenched! I studied, I competed and I taught. The more I taught, the better student I became and the better student I became, the more I wanted to teach. As I advanced in belt rank, and before I knew it, I was teaching private lessons to lower belt ranks. Then one day it occurred to me... I had finally become a teacher!

About this same time I discovered Jack Canfield's work on self-esteem and I started reading and listening to everything of his that I could get my hands on. His words really spoke to me and I realized that the only limitations I had were the limitations I had placed on myself. I was like a phoenix rising from the ashes. I began to discover who I was and realize the strength of my mind. I started using this new found knowledge in my Martial Arts career during competitions and sparring.

Finally I realized that knowing how to fight meant *that I did not need to fight.* My quest to learn Martial Arts was to get rid of all of the anger I was holding on to from my childhood. I also wanted the opportunity for just one person to try to take advantage of me again so that I could defend myself. Martial Arts taught me peace of mind and I no longer felt the need to withdraw into my world of fantasy where I could control a situation with my fighting abilities. I was learning to fight with my mind and let go of my fear.

Chocolate or Vanilla

Chapter 15

During this time an event happened that changed the course of my life. I was at work and my daughter called me. She was crying. I started to panic and I asked her what was wrong. She was crying and she said, "Mama, daddy is really mad and he started kicking me all the way across the living room and I don't know what to do and he hurt me."

Physical abuse was not something she had ever dealt with and this was inexcusable. I talked very calmly to her and asked her to put her dad on the phone. When he got on the phone I don't remember what I said but I was so angry and upset. My beautiful daughter, that I vowed would never know violence in her life, had just suffered physical abuse from her father and I was not there to protect her. I knew I had to discuss what had happened with my husband and that he needed to deal with his anger. I had to know that I would never have to worry again that he might take his anger out on my daughter.

The discussion started like so many times before. He was angry and I knew from his body language that he didn't want to talk about it. He never wanted to talk; he always just wanted the incident to go away. We needed to talk about what he did to our daughter and I needed to know that it would never happen again.

As I started talking, he was sitting on the edge of the bed and his back was to me and the more I tried to talk to him the more agitated his body language became. Then he started pounding his fists on either side of him, as though the mattress was a drum, and he continued pounding on the mattress. *Immediately I sensed that this was a situation far worse than I had ever dealt with before.*

I felt the urgency to diffuse the situation so I decided to get up and walk away for awhile so that he would have a chance to calm down until we could talk. As soon as I walked in front of him he stood up, grabbed me by the shoulders and physically threw me into a set of mirrored closet doors. I hit the doors with such force I do not know why they didn't shatter into a million pieces. As the back of my head hit the mirrors my immediate thought was "this can't be happening, he can't mean this, this is a mistake, and, how can I help him?" But when I landed on my feet and stood facing him I saw fire in his eyes and spit coming out of his mouth.

My self-defense instincts kicked in and I knew that I did not want to try to run out of the bedroom door because I might make too much noise if he came after me and I did not want to wake my girls. That is when my resolve to stand my ground came into focus. I stepped into a defensive stance, held up my hand in a "stop" motion and said, "Stop right there. If you come any closer I am prepared to send you flying out the window behind you."

Suddenly recognition returned to his face and he was immediately sorry for what he had done. For me, he had gone past the point of no return. Now what? Looking back, I know that was the night my marriage ended and yet it would take 13 more years of believing that I was doing the "right thing" by staying committed to my marriage before the marriage finally ended in divorce. Yes, he went to counseling and yes, I even went with him. But counseling only works when you are committed to change. The definition of insanity is doing the

Chocolate or Vanilla

same thing over and over and expecting different results.

Chocolate or Vanilla

"Men feel threatened by women; because they are afraid women will laugh at them." "Women feel threatened by men because they're afraid of being killed." - Gavin De Becker

Chapter 16

When I was young and wanted to dissociate from a situation I would dream about fighting back and coming out the victor! When I started Martial Arts, I continued to disassociate during situations where I felt I was under attack until I felt empowered enough to no longer need these fantasy daydreams. Whatever gets you through the events in which you feel least empowered, use it to your advantage and understand that this is your Inner Strength showing you "the way" to empowerment.

I have always said that parenting does not come with a manual. How do you know if you are being a good parent, an effective parent, and making the right choices? All I had to guide me was my heart and my heart told me that as long as my daughters felt safe and secure, they would have the strength to be or do anything they wanted. I enrolled them in the Karate studio with me so that they could have the benefit of the Martial Arts.

As a mother I gained so much more by having them in the dojo with me every day. I was very fortunate to have men in the studio that respected my quest for knowledge. These men worked beside me and became my best friends and watched over my daughters. It was the best feeling a mother could have to know that these guys not only had my back, but were also watching out for my daughters. My fellow students came from all walks of life and we studied, trained, and competed side by side. We cheered each other on in tournaments and we were there for each other when one of us needed a friend to lean on.

I watched my daughters grow into secure young women and I was proud of them and of my success as a mother. I never understood when I would hear parents say, "I can't wait until my children grow up and move out." I loved every minute that I spent with my daughters and while I knew that one day they would eventually move out into the world, I treasured every day we spent together.

Chocolate or Vanilla

Chapter 17

My parenting beliefs were put to the test soon after my oldest daughter graduated from high school. She told me she was pregnant, and she cried because she was so scared. I took her in my arms, held her close to me, told her that I loved her, and that I will always be there for her. Knowing how much work it is to be a parent, I knew that my daughter needed me more at that time than possibly any other time in her life.

By this time my youngest daughter was studying to be a nurse and when my oldest daughter went into labor, both me and my youngest daughter were in the delivery room with her. As I stood at her head helping her breathe through every contraction, the doctor commented on how amazed she was that I was able to keep my daughter so calm. We were quite a team and we worked together. When my grandson finally decided to push his way into this world I almost choked up with emotion but my youngest daughter nudged me in the ribs with her elbow as if to say, "you have come this far mom, don't lose it now." It was her strength that empowered me to be strong enough for her sister.

My grandson was born and, true to my word, I worked side by side with my daughter to raise him for the first 9 ½ years of his life. He is such a gift and I finally understood the phrase: "if I had known grandchildren were so much fun, I would have had them first!" Once again I was blessed with another child in my life and I thank my daughter every day for the wonderful gift she has given me.

Chapter 18

One of the things we are taught in Karate is how to fall and roll while protecting your body and your head. This served me well in July 2005, when I fell and broke both ankle bones in my left leg. I managed to protect my head AND the coffee cup I was carrying but my leg took the brunt of the fall. I broke both ankle bones in my left leg which resulted in surgery, a five day stay in the hospital, 4 months in a wheelchair, then a walker, and gradually using a cane to walk again. Being confined to a wheelchair was almost more than I could bear. I was in such pain and I could not do anything on my own. I believe that everything happens for a reason but at that time my faith in that belief was really put to the test. I could not find one positive reason for being stuck in that wheelchair.

By May of 2006 I was still using a cane and walking was very painful for me. In the meantime I had gained so much weight and, hard as I tried to get rid of the excess fat that I was carrying around, nothing seemed to work. That same month I was introduced to the Isagenix Cleansing and Fat Burning System that is the basis of the nutrition system I still use today. Because Isagenix is distributed through a multilevel marketing plan, the person that signed me up wanted me to start a business, but I wanted no part of another MLM company.

Towards the end of July I received another box of products in the mail and there was a flyer in the box advertising the upcoming annual seminar for Isagenix. Although I wanted to continue to improve my health, I was not the least bit interested in attending the seminar. Past experience had turned me against the thought of an MLM business. I threw the flyer on the table and when it landed, it flipped over. On the back of the flyer was an announcement for the upcoming seminar and it showed the guest speaker… the guest speaker was none other than Jack Canfield!!!

Oh my gosh, I was so excited, here was an opportunity to hear Jack Canfield speak in person! I called my friend and told her that we needed to attend the seminar and my only goal was to get the opportunity to listen to Jack Canfield speak. Finally the day arrived. It was an hour before Jack was scheduled to be on stage, so I told my friend that we needed to find a seat. I had my camera ready to take his picture and I was very excited. As the escalator at Mandalay Bay carried us up to the top floor I looked to my left and could not believe my eyes. "Look, there is Jack Canfield," I said to my friend. "He is standing by that table with all of his books and there isn't anyone around him. Let's go see if I can shake his hand and get a picture with him." My friend and I walked up to Jack and as he turned to greet me, I put out my hand to shake his hand and introduce myself. To my horror, all that came out was a flood of tears.

The emotional release from everything I had learned since being introduced to Jack Canfield's work, all of my work in Martial Arts, and the past year of trying to walk again came washing over me like a tidal wave and all I could do was stand there and cry. I cried so hard I could barely breathe and all I could think about was, "Oh great, I finally get an opportunity to meet Jack Canfield and tell him what an impact his work has had on me and all I can do is stand here and cry; he must think I am an idiot! But then I thought of something. I thought that if Jack really believed in what he taught, he wouldn't think I am an idiot. Nonetheless I was so frustrated with myself because all I could do was stand there, holding his hand, and crying.

Just then my friend spoke up and saved the day. She looked at Jack and said, "You have had quite an impact on her life and she was truly looking forward to meeting you." And then Jack said, "I can see that." Turning to me, Jack said, "It's ok. You obviously have something very important to say to me, I will wait."

I could not believe it. As I glanced behind me I noticed a line beginning to form with other people that wanted to talk to Jack. Jack noticed me looking at the line that was forming behind me and said, "I allow a certain amount of time to speak with people before I give a talk. I don't always get to talk to everyone in the line but I take the time to make sure that the people I do get to talk to have my attention.

It seemed like 10 minutes or more that Jack waited for me to gain my composure long enough to be able to talk. As I finally gained my composure, I nodded my head, took a deep breath, and said, "thank you for all of your work. You have made such a difference in my life. Can I get a picture with you?" So Jack posed for a picture with me and I carry it with me to this day as a reminder that nothing is impossible if you believe and ask for what you want. You may not get what you want in the way you envisioned it, but you will get what you want or something better!

Chapter 19

My health was improving every day; I was walking better and had decided to build an Isagenix business after all! My life has been truly abundant and I have found that many people do not understand true wealth. You can go after the money and you might get rich, but that isn't necessarily wealth. Happiness doesn't necessarily mean getting the material things; what we truly want is happiness. Concentrate on what makes you happy and you will be wealthier than you ever imagined possible.

In 2008 I had a second surgery to have the plate and screws removed from my leg. Not long after my second surgery my husband of 34 years asked me to file for divorce. I felt as though the bottom had fallen out of my world and my world, as I knew it, came to a standstill. How was I going to move forward, face my children, my friends, or myself?

Chocolate or Vanilla

Everything I had known for the last 36 years was rapidly changing and my life was totally out of control. I had always felt a huge sense of accomplishment for being married for so long and it was a big part of who I was. I was sad and confused. Even though I knew that my marriage was not healthy for either of us, I wanted desperately to hold on to the only security I had managed to build in my life. I wanted him to want our marriage to be better. I wanted to keep my commitment to my marriage. But just as much, I wanted to be free of this toxic relationship. I did not know how to free myself from the relationship and stay committed to my marriage. I was so tired of living a lie and trying to keep up appearances of a happy marriage. Friends used to tell me that I was so lucky because I had a nice house, beautiful daughters, and from their perception, the ideal marriage. I heard a quote from Jerry Lewis once where he said "people can compliment you on your new shoes, but only you know how much they hurt your feet!" My life had always included my quest for being the best "me" I could be and my husband's quest involved sitting in front of the TV.

I did not have the first clue about where to start in filing for a divorce but I had the "Inner Strength" to find out. How do you separate the last 36 years with someone? During our marriage my husband wanted nothing to do with our finances and household decisions were left up to me. Now I was being faced with another decision and did not know where to start. One day I looked around my house and said to myself, "Well, the best place to start is with the truth!" So I called a friend, explained what was happening, asked her if she and her husband would be willing to rent a room to me, and then I went to the bookstore and bought a book titled *How to File for Divorce in California* (later I found out there is a website that has all of the necessary paperwork/forms you will need. You can Google the information for the website that will have the necessary paperwork for your area). I knew it was up to me to make this happen so I started filling out paperwork, going to the courthouse, filing paperwork, making mistakes, redoing paperwork, and making more mistakes. I learned from every mistake.

I teach my students that a mistake is a great opportunity to learn a better way. In the movies, when they are shooting a scene they may have to film it numerous times before they get it right. I am sure you have seen where they say "Action, take one." Then they shoot it again and say "Action, take two." I like to call this a mis-take. This gives it a positive spin because it allows you the opportunity for a re-take, over and over until you get it the way you want it! If you take a picture and you aren't happy with the results, you can take it again until you get the look you want! Believe me when I say "I had many mis-takes while filing my divorce papers."

I knew if I was going to start a New Beginning that I had to move out of my home, out of my comfort zone – no regrets and no looking back.

The day I moved out of my house I didn't care if I took anything with me. All I wanted was to move out with my bed, my pillow, my clothes and my computer. Thankfully my brother and my friends were looking out for me and know me well. My books are such an important part of my life. When my friend started packing them up I told her to just leave them. She said "Miss Nancy, I know you, I know how important your books are to you and we are taking these books with us." She packed up all of my books and helped move me into my rented room.

I cried many tears during my divorce because I felt as though I had failed at the one thing I set out to do right in my life, to be a good mom, wife, and homemaker. How could I possibly be a good mom when I was getting a divorce, moving out of the home where I had raised my children and my grandson? I felt as though I was walking through jello and that my life had no direction.

I lost everything, and then something amazing happened. I found myself!

Chapter 20

During my divorce, being surrounded by people that truly loved me and wanted me to succeed, who believed in me as much as I believed in myself, gave me the strength I needed during those times when I thought I could not make it through one more day. I didn't just lose my home; I lost the only safe haven I have ever known.

This above all, refuse to be a victim.

— Margaret Atwood

Chapter 21

Something amazing happened when I filed for divorce; my mother came into my life. Since my mother had been absent most of my life, I was a little surprised to get a call from her one day. She asked "is there something I should know?" I really didn't see why I should have to go into the mess I was going through regarding my divorce, but I also had no reason not to answer her question. So I told her the truth; "I had filed for divorce." She then asked me what had happened and I gave her a brief summary. "Nancy," she said, "I have not been there for you your whole life. All of your life you have had to take care of everyone else. Please give me the chance to be there for you now while you are going through this."

WOW, who was this woman and what had she done with my mother? I was speechless and didn't know what to say. That was mostly because never having had her in my life meant that I didn't even know where to start to let her help me. So we just took it one day at a time. Every day we would talk on the phone and she would ask me how I was doing. She would always tell me that she loved me and that she was there for me. She even bought a cell phone and learned how to text so she could stay in touch and send me messages throughout the day letting me know she was thinking of me and that she was behind me 100%!

During this process my mother and the man she had been seeing for the past 36 years got married to each other. I can't begin to understand her 36 year journey with this man and the choices they decided to make to be together while each of them were married to someone else. I do know that her choices have given her insight to be there for me when I seemed to have needed her the most. And for that I am grateful. We have many years to make up for and have begun working together to support each other.

Recently my mother asked me a question. "Nancy, how can I make it up to you? How can I go back and undo what I have done?" My answer was, "Ma, you can't undo the past. All we can do is leave the past in the past, learn from our mis-takes, honor

Chocolate or Vanilla

each other in the present and we will build a better 'us' in the future!"

Chapter 22

The hours waiting for my divorce turned into days and the days turned into weeks and the weeks turned into months. By the time my divorce was final I had turned my attention to my home based business. I made a promise to myself that I would never again be dependent on someone else for my financial well being. My business started giving me the financial freedom I needed and I hired a life coach. I chose the perfect name for my business "New Beginnings with Nancy" and, being the most positive person I know, I chose to take a leap of faith, quit my corporate job and work my business. I am now able to fulfill my purpose which is to use my optimism and positive outlook to be a beacon for others to find the way to their Inner Strength!

Dealing with the divorce, the ups and downs during the entire process, gaining the support from my mother, and my own self growth has given me new insight into who I am. There really is life after divorce and knowing who you are is the most valuable tool you can possess. You have to know who you are before you can know what you want in your life.

Chapter 23

As a professional speaker, I teach self-defense techniques during my speaking engagements. When I am speaking in front of an audience and I teach a self-defense technique to a woman and watch her feel empowered as she realizes her "Inner Strength," when I watch her master the technique that she did not realize she possessed, I feel like doing the "happy dance." I then tell her, "Just imagine, you walked in here not knowing that you already possessed the "Inner Strength" to master this technique. What other knowledge or ability do you hold inside you that you do not realize you possess? The possibilities are endless!"

You can be anything you want to be, there are no limits. By believing in myself, I have given myself permission to find out who I really am. I came to realize that I had been living my life like Clark Kent, going around hiding who I really am and now I have removed the disguise and showed the world that I am actually Superman. I am a beacon of light that shines brightly for others to follow. My "Inner Strength" is a gift and I want to share this gift. In fact, I promise you, if you have taken the time to read my story, I truly believe you have the gift of "Inner Strength" inside you and I would love to know how I can support you towards "the way" to your New Beginnings!

Henry Ford said "Whether you think you can, or whether you think you can't, you are probably right!"

If you begin with the end in mind (the end being where you want to be) how can you possibly fail? I work with entrepreneurial women and the "Have It All" woman who understands that in order for her to "have it all" she must first take care of herself.

Taking care of yourself also means taking care of your health. You can have everything you ever dreamed of, but if you do not have your health, you will not be around to enjoy the fruits of your labor. Health is also important because your health is your first line of self-defense.

I truly believe that when the student is ready, the teacher will appear. I am passionate about sharing my life experiences with others in the hope that something I have learned or experienced will, in

Chocolate or Vanilla

some way, help someone else that is facing a challenge so daunting that she might not realize she has the "Inner Strength" to turn her life around.

Chapter 24

The definition of insanity is continuing to make the same choices, over and over, and expect different results. If you can work past appearances to get to the truth and deal with whatever you are avoiding, the truth shall set you free!

> Knowing others is wisdom, knowing yourself is Enlightenment.
>
> – Lao-Tzu

What is holding you back?

Empty Your Cup

There are times in our life when we will have to unlearn all that we have learned so that we can start learning all over again. Bruce Lee used to tell this story... It is about a Japanese Zen master who received a university professor who came to inquire about Zen.

"It was obvious to the master from the start of the conversation that the professor was not so much interested in learning about Zen as he was in impressing the master with his own opinions and knowledge. The master listened patiently and finally suggested they have tea. The master poured his visitor's cup full and then kept on pouring.

The professor watched the cup overflowing until he could no longer restrain himself and said, "The cup is overfull, no more will go in."

The master replied, "Like this cup, you are full of your own opinions and speculations. How can I show you Zen unless you first empty your cup?"

The meaning is clear... we must empty our mind of past knowledge and old habits so that we will be open to new learning.

- Zen in the Martial Arts

Chapter 25

I learned to ask myself if I was holding myself back because of past experiences or beliefs. How were these past experiences or beliefs serving me? If they were not serving me, how could I learn to let them go? What were my relationships like? Did I hang around people that empowered me or did I hang around with people that were going nowhere fast? Like attracts like, so I looked for the people that were doing what I wanted to do and found a way to be involved in similar experiences.

I found a mentor, someone that was doing what I wanted to do and was successful doing it. I learned to incorporate similar experiences into my life. Often family and friends I had known for years were the people that held me back the most because they saw me as that same person they had known for so many years. It was difficult for them to understand my journey and they (consciously or unconsciously) tried to hold me back because they were unable to give me the support I required.

I also asked myself "Where did my focus lie?" I learned that often we can have our eye on a specific goal and we are so focused on reaching that specific goal that we miss the many opportunities along the way. When one eye is fixed upon our destination, there is only one eye left with which to find "the way." Or worse, if both eyes are fixed upon a destination you may miss the many signs along the way for a better opportunity or a better way to reach your destination.

Once I discovered my goals, I wrote them down and asked myself "What was I doing on a daily basis to bring me closer to my goals?" I used the word "SMART" when considering my goals. SMART stands for **S**pecific, **M**easurable, **A**ttainable, **R**easonable, and **T**imely.

Keeping in mind that vague goals bring vague results, I learned to make my goals clear. For instance, if my goal was "I want to lose about 30 pounds in the next few months," this was not a goal, this was a wish. A SMART Goal would sound like this: I will lose 30 pounds in the next 6 months or sooner by eating nutritious foods and exercising 4 times a week. Here is another example: Financial independence is important to me and so is time freedom. I chose these two areas to attract into my life so that when I wake up every morning I can choose how to spend the day and have the financial freedom to follow my passion.

I listed my top 9 core values in my "I love me journal" and refer to them every day to stay on track.

By core values, I mean the beliefs that are so strong within me that I will do whatever it takes to live by them. For instance, my core values are:

1. Positive Energy/Attitude
2. Vibrant Health
3. Time / Financial Freedom
4. Making a difference through contribution
5. Quest for knowledge
6. Not being attached to the outcome / living in the "now"
7. Reciprocity in my relationships; Family, Partner, Friends
8. Fun & Adventure; living my life to the fullest
9. Personal/Spiritual Growth

Chapter 26

High school was not a memorable time for me; my school had just been built and most of the kids came from families that had a lot of money. I had no money, my clothes were not in fashion, I was always hungry and I had a hard time with my classes because learning did not come easy for me. I never seemed to understand how to study for a test and prayed for at least a "C" on every test. My classmates seemed to breeze through tests and classes while I always seemed to have a mental block when it came to studying.

I had never attended any of my high school reunions, mostly because it just didn't seem that important to me and felt no reason to dwell on my high school days. I had moved forward with my life and a reunion simply seemed like going backwards to me. When I received an invitation for my 25th high school reunion my Aunt Judy asked me if I was going to attend. I told her that I was not planning to attend and she asked me "why." I tried to explain to her that high school did not hold good memories for me. If you attend a school that has a lot of money and you don't have money it can be tough. I was always begging dimes from people and once I would collect 10 dimes I could eat a pretty good lunch.

I told Aunt Judy that I was always so hungry and I was always bumming dimes from people. I told her I didn't want to go to the reunion and be reminded that I was always asking people for dimes." To which my Aunt Judy replied, "Oh for heaven sake, take a bag of dimes and go!"

That was some of the best advice I have ever gotten. I followed her advice and went to the reunion (without the bag of dimes) and to my surprise, no one brought up anything about money. I had many people tell me that they remembered how kind I was, or how thoughtful I was or how I was the only person that used to talk to them on the bus. It was my *"positive"* that they remembered, not my *"negative"*! So the next time you have a limiting belief that is holding you back, my advice to you would be "take a bag of dimes and go!"

I started by asking myself 3 simple questions:

1. Is there anything I would like to change about my "self?"
2. Is there anything I would like to change about my "health?"
3. Is there anything I would like to change about my "wealth?"

If I answered "yes" to any of these 3 questions, then I had a good starting place. I can be the most positive person or the wealthiest person, but if my health is not where it should be, how can I possibly expect to grow my "self" or my "wealth"? Then I asked myself "What would a New Beginning in these three areas look like to me?"

Chapter 27

I learned how important it was to discover my purpose in life. Your purpose in life is that which brings you the greatest joy. For instance, my purpose in life is "to use my optimism and positive outlook to be a beacon for others to find the way to their Inner Strength!" You will know when you are living your purpose because of how you feel. Living your purpose makes you feel good and if you find a way to live your purpose and you can earn a living doing it, you will never work another day in your life!

I paid attention to my self-talk. Your self-talk is that voice inside your head that speaks to you as soon as someone else stops speaking to you. For instance, if I tell you that you have on a nice piece of jewelry, do you say to yourself, "yes, I am very proud of this piece?" Or do you say, "oh no, I knew I should have worn the other piece of jewelry because it matches my outfit so much better. Why did she have to comment on this jewelry, does she really think it looks nice or is she just saying that?" You see, it isn't what I say to you that matters, it's what you say to yourself once I stop speaking.

Paying close attention to my self-talk gave me a better grasp on my belief in myself.

I keep an "I love me" journal and write down the positive things that happen in my daily life. You will be surprised at how good you will feel about yourself when you can read the abundance that is being drawn into your life. When you are feeling low, reading this journal can pick you up faster than anything that anyone can say to you because you will be reading your own positive experiences!

I created a "vision board." A vision board is a very powerful tool to move you towards your goals. It can be as elaborate or as simple as you want it to be. I started out with a poster board and cut out pictures of things from magazines or the internet I wanted to attract into my life. For instance, if you want a new washer and dryer, find a picture of the exact model you would like, and cut it out and paste it to your vision board.

Fill your vision board up with as many things as you can fit onto the poster board. Hang it somewhere where you can see it every day to remind you of what you want to attract into your life. You don't have to know *HOW* you are going to attract it, you only have to know *WHAT* you want to attract. When you concentrate on what you want, you will attract it or something better into your life. I wanted to travel to Japan so I cut out pictures of places in Japan and within 2 years the opportunity to travel to Japan was offered to me. I ended up visiting every single place in Japan that I had cut out and pasted on my vision board!

I stopped making excuses! I found that I was setting goals only to find that I was not achieving them and then offering excuses as to "why" I hadn't achieved them. I had to be honest with myself because if I was not honest with myself, I couldn't be honest with others. Sometimes I discovered goals that I thought were so important just weren't as important as I thought they were. I also discovered that I hadn't put in the necessary work needed to achieve certain goals. Either way, if I made excuses I was not being honest with myself.

I looked at my relationships to see if I was hanging around with positive people that lifted me up or was I hanging around toxic people? Toxic people are those people that never seem to have anything positive to say or try to bring your positive mood down to their level of negativity. Toxic people may not know they are toxic and if you try to explain it to them, they probably won't get what you are talking about. They just do what they always do and it never occurs to them to move forward or think "outside of the box." When you are around toxic people do you find yourself remaining positive or being dragged down to their level? There were people in my life that were toxic and I had to limit or eliminate my time with them. Remember, it may not be about you. If you can't have the relationship that you want with a parent or someone in your life, it may not have anything to do with you. Maybe it is about them and their struggle. All you have control over is you and the thoughts you think.

I used to try to control situations to keep my world in order because I felt it was the best way to keep people from taking advantage of me. I had to learn to let go of the outcome! I have found that when I try to force someone or a situation, it usually isn't meant to be! Bill Mayer teaches: "My thoughts control my life, my questions control my thoughts. When I master my questions, I will master my life!" This is a great philosophy to live by.

Chapter 28

I asked myself, "what was I avoiding?" This was brutal because I answered "yes" to each one of these questions...

1. Do you feel the need to remove your shoes and your belt before getting on the scale at the doctor's office?
2. Do you hate shopping for clothes because an extra large doesn't seem large enough?
3. Do you blame the dryer for clothes that have become too tight on you?
4. Do you dread going out because you feel you have nothing to wear that makes you feel good about yourself?
5. Do you try to eat right but always feel hungry?
6. Do you feel like you have tried every diet on the planet?

7. Have you considered surgery to get into shape?
8. Have you ever wished you weighed MORE so that you would qualify for weight loss surgery?
9. Have you ever wished you weighed LESS so you would qualify for weight loss surgery?
10. Do you no longer believe there is any way for you to get rid of your excess fat?
11. When you go shopping do you choose shoes, jewelry and purses because you know they will "always fit?"
12. Do you look forward to getting home at the end of the day so you can change into looser clothing?
13. Do you have challenges walking because your legs hurt and you know that if you got rid of some extra pounds that your legs would probably feel better?
14. Do you take medication due to weight related challenges?
15. Are you afraid of getting diabetes due to weight related issues?
16. Are you convinced that you are "big boned?"
17. Do you worry about passing your weight issues on to your children?
18. Are you continually out of energy?
19. Do you hate having your picture taken?

20. Do you find yourself constantly making jokes about your weight before anyone else can mention it first?
21. Do you wish you could make friends with your mirror?

I had to be totally truthful with myself in order to deal with whatever I was avoiding. Stress, depression, poor health, allergies, migraines, hopelessness, and fear are symptoms, not problems. These are toxic to the body – get them out of you and start living in a state of wellness! Tears shed in sorrow or grief emit different chemicals than tears shed from happiness and joy.

CRYING CAN BE GOOD!

It is important for women to be self-preserving and to put themselves first. If you are a mother this is a hard concept to grasp because we moms always feel the need to put our children first. But think of it this way: when the flight attendant is explaining what to do if the cabin should suddenly lose pressure and the oxygen mask drops in front of you, they always tell you to put your mask on first and then put the mask on your children. Think about it… if you put their mask on first, and you pass out, you will be no good to your children. The same holds true with whatever you are doing in

Chocolate or Vanilla

your life. If you are worn out and tired, you are no good to yourself or to anyone else. Take care of your body and your body will take care of you.

Chapter 29

I am moving forward with my life and letting my light shine bright for all to see, that I might be a beacon for others to follow if they are looking for the "Inner Strength" to find their own light.

My life has taken a new path towards my passion to empower other women by sharing my life experiences in the hope that something I have experienced or learned will give them the courage they need to take that first step on their path to a New Beginning to find their Inner Strength.

Watch for me; I might be the speaker at your next event or the tour guide on your next vacation and then you can say "hey, that's Nancy; I read her story. If she can be up there on stage… so can I!"

Here is your opportunity to grab a bag of dimes and go.

Chocolate or Vanilla

So what's it going to be… vanilla or chocolate? I will have a scoop of each, please!

Resources:

- Jack Canfield; The Success Principles, How to Build High Self Esteem
- Jeff Olson; The slight Edge
- Joe Hyams; Zen in the Martial Arts
- Don Millman; Way of the Peaceful Warrior
- Don Miguel Ruiz; The 4 Agreements
- Robert Kiyosaki; Rich Dad Poor Dad
- Paul Zane Pilzer; The New Wellness Revolution
- Gavin DeBecker; The Gift of Fear
- Napoleon Hill; Think and Grow Rich
- Rhonda Byrne; The Secret
- Steven R Covey; 7 Habits of Highly Effective people
- Bill Mayer; The Magic in Asking The Right Questions
- Viktor Frankl; Man's Search for Meaning
- Jim Rohn; Building Your Network Marketing Business
- Jim Rohn; Challenge to Succeed
- T. Harv Eker; Secrets of the Millionaire Mind
- Wayne Dyer; Manifest Your Destiny
- Caroline Myss; Finding Your Sacred Contract

EPILOGUE

As a child, when our TV show was over, my mother would tell us to turn off the TV but I would always say, "wait ma, we have to see the epilogue." I think it only fitting to share this epilogue with you, as it is a note that my mother emailed to me after reading my book. This epilogue is word for word...

Nancy,
I want to tell you how much I enjoyed reading your book. I've learned a lot from just reading it as it opened so many secrets that I kept hidden all these years as everything was so painful and embarrassing to bring forward as one could never believe what I would have to tell them from the day I married. I was a young innocent child taken right to the "snake pit". It broke my heart each day with each child I brought into the world to be subjected to him and our life. How could I have acted so badly with you children as I loved each one of you so much, and I know now that each of you were hurt so badly in so many ways. Why did I contribute to your hurts?
I spent 16 years with him so you know how many ugly secrets I have hidden.
Your book has opened many doors and thoughts for me and a new life. I feel freed after reading your book, and I want to read it over and over, I am free. Does that make sense?
Love you,
Mom

P. S. Who would have thought your book would have helped me the most!

Chocolate or Vanilla

I would love to hear about your experiences with Chocolate or Vanilla; Life Is All About Choices.

Please feel free to contact me at
nancy@newbeginningswithnancy.com

You can also write me at:
    Nancy Hirschman
    New Beginnings with Nancy
    PO Box 9838
    Fountain Valley, Ca 92728

Printed in the United States

www.ingramcontent.com/pod-product-compliance
Lightning Source LLC
Chambersburg PA
CBHW071728040426
42446CB00011B/2263